The Art Of Cryptocurrency

Beginner's tool to understanding the world of cryptocurrency

Copyright © 2018 by William B. Skates

All right reserved. No portion of this book may be reproduced, stored in a retrieval system, or transmitted in any form or by any means – electronic, mechanical, recording or otherwise – except for brief quotation in printed reviews without the prior written permission of the publisher or the author.

Table of Contents

INTRODUCTION 4
CHAPTER ONE 7
   Cryptocurrency: what is it? 7
CHAPTER TWO 15
   An introduction to the types of cryptocurrencies 15
CHAPTER THREE 24
   Top Steps on how to Invest in Cryptocurrency 24
CHAPTER FOUR 39
   How to protect and share Cryptocurrency 39
      The Best Wallets to Keep your Coins Safe 40
   The best ways to share your crypto coins 46
CHAPTER FIVE 48
   Introduction to Mining 48
CHAPTER SIX 54
   The future of Cryptocurrency 54
CONCLUSION 61

Get Your Free Gift

Are you interested in learning more about Bitcoin and how to start investing, buying or mining with no technical background or experience in the world of day trading? You are on the right place!

I giveaway this report that reveals everything you need to know to start making an extra income with Bitcoin! The report won't be up forever, so get it before it's taken down. It's my simple way of saying thank you for reading my book. https://www.subscribepage.com/bitcoin-for-beginners

Download one of the BEST Reports **ABSOLUTELY FREE** that will help you learn more about Bitcoin mining!

Introduction

When I look around the world today, I see a hub filled with great opportunities for people who are willing to grab them with both hands. No one should ever have to complain about a lack of finance because what I'm about to introduce to you is currently the most trending item in the world of finance. I want you to get so excited about this because if you thought you had heard it all about being prosperous digitally, then you haven't heard anything at all. This book was written with some goals in mind; I hope that when you get to the last chapter, you can categorically say that I accomplished my mission and you are much better than you were when you started reading.

The first goal for me is to enlighten you on the possibilities that lie within engaging in digital currencies and the second goal is to help you take definite steps towards reaping the benefits that come with cryptocurrency. I am aware that there is a myriad of information out there on cryptocurrencies, you probably gave up because no one could narrow down the concept for you, but I have good news for you, after reading this book, your understanding will be enlightened. You will know everything (from A-Z) on cryptocurrency. You will gain so much knowledge broken down into simpler forms that you wouldn't have to feel lost again. I want you to know that this book was written for you!

I thought about the young investor who didn't know the steps to take, I thought about the stay home mum who needed a more diversified financial portfolio, and I thought about the young man/woman who needs to make more money for the future. It doesn't matter the category you fall into, be rest assured that this book has got you covered. I have only one request as we sail on in this journey to infinite wealth and that is your proactivity. Learning and implementing are two different things entirely; you can learn and not put the knowledge to good use, or you can learn and get the value of what you paid for. So I implore you to take strategic steps towards bringing the words you read about life.

Alright, enough of the small talk already, let's get started and let's begin now. The first chapter explores the meaning of cryptocurrency; what is it about? What do we do with it? How is it shaping our world? What role do you play in its evolution? Get ready to receive answers to these and much more; you are about to embark on the most exciting and value-added journey ever, ready? Let us begin.

Chapter One

Cryptocurrency: what is it?

Cryptocurrency is a digital medium of exchange through which information is shared using cryptography; this is the process of converting data into a code. The brief definition provided above should create an image of a currency that is backed by the assurance of technology. This also explains the role cryptography plays; since cryptocurrency is security driven, cryptography ensures that it is protected thus making it difficult for hackers to create a counterfeit. Think of it as a digital currency that helps you do whatever you want to in a fast, reliable and trustworthy way all in a world that has embraced the importance of technology

The most beautiful about this currency lies in the fact that you can sit in the comfort of your home and trade with it, buy, invest and do whatever you want to without actually waiting on the physical material. Cryptocurrencies can be transferred between peers and then confirmed in a ledger that is public through a process known as mining. Once a transaction is confirmed, the information is stored in the public ledger; the essence of this is to track the coins and ensure that it is spent by the owner of the coin. This process of identifying the owner of coins and the public ledger is referred to as the transaction block chain. As we progress, I will be sharing some fundamental concepts about cryptocurrencies that will help you gain an understanding of what cryptocurrency is about. These pieces of information will also help you get used to some of the crypto terminologies you will encounter.

The next thing you should know is this; there are different types of cryptocurrencies in the world today, we will highlight the various forms as we move on. Most of these currencies are controlled by a centralized government as such there is always a third party that regulates their creation, what this means is that the process of creating cryptocurrency is an open one that is usually controlled by a code and ultimately relies on a peer-to-peer network. So the system works when individuals trade off it. Now, where do owners of crypto coins keep their digital coins?

Owners of crypto coins keep their coins in an encrypted digital wallet. You can open a digital wallet with any recognized and safe cryptocurrency platform as such; it provides a safe place where you can purchase your coins and store them till you are ready to invest with them. Your cryptocurrency wallet works with a password and for you to keep it secure, you need to be sure that the password is strong enough, do not share the password with someone else and do not use a password that can be susceptible to hackers as well. Remember that despite the fact that we are dealing with a digital currency doesn't mean you should relax, be informed about everything and take the necessary precautions to protecting your wallet and accounts.

Next, we will be learning about the value of crypto coins, how valuable are these coins? For a currency to be recognized, it has to have some form of benefit. Stick with me as I break down the value chain of cryptocurrency. First, cryptocurrency is in the way of coins, and they are produced by miners. Miners are individuals who operate programs on unique hardware, the process of mining these coins adds value to them. More so, the scarcity of coins and their subsequent demand causes a spike in the fluctuating amount of coins. Think about the stock market in the country and how shares go up and come down; this process highlights how volatile shares are and how they can be unpredictable. The same thing applies to cryptocurrencies; for you to get the most out of this emerging market, you have to study the times and seasons of the coins.

At this point, you might still experience confusion with regards the terms and how the digital coins work but don't worry about it. People learn at a different pace as such; you don't have to feel bad for not getting it all at once. This book is yours now so feel free to come back to it at anything and read through for guidance. The primary trick with cryptocurrency is the fact that you are always learning new facts and details as the days go by. So the key is staying updated all the time; after reading this book and getting empowered, the next stop is never stopped learning materials that are related to this. Keep searching and keep on reading, the more you know, the better your chances at investing and making a profit.

Currently, you can use cryptocurrency in some ways aside from trading. At inception, it wasn't so, you could only buy, keep it in your wallet and trade at the peak points, but things are changing quickly. First, it started with online retail stores accepting the most popular form of cryptocurrency called the "Bitcoin" (we will learn more about this in the next chapter) but now, stores online, and some offline accept crypto coins. The more awareness and attention the digital currencies get, the more viable and acceptable it is to organizations and companies. So you don't have to worry if the digital coins are accepted, learn as much as you can and your knowledge will lead you to wealth someday.

This chapter has been an introduction into the world of cryptocurrency. You have learnt the meaning, how it is gotten, where it is kept, and the possibility for profit maximization as well as the potential it holds in our present world. With this information, it is safe to say that you are ready for the next phase of this journey which is an introduction to the various types of cryptocurrencies currently available in the market. You will find out all about this and much more in the next chapter, ready to add to your knowledge base? Let's do this!

Chapter Two
An introduction to the types of cryptocurrencies

There are various types of cryptocurrencies out there on the market. Although the Bitcoin is the most popular of them all, I want you to know that there are several others you can also utilize. This chapter serves as an introduction to the types of crypto coins available for use. It is essential that you have this information at your fingertips because, as the cryptocurrency market expands, you get more and more options so why restrict yourself to just one when you have a myriad of opportunities to work with. There is a caveat though, before trading with a crypto coin, carry7 out research on the coin and get to know everything about it especially, its volatility and acceptance.

The reason Bitcoin has been largely successful is due to the fact that it was accepted by a wide range of people from inception Some cryptocurrencies still struggle with such level of acceptability But all hope isn't lost, keep your knowledge updated and you will get to know the coins that are soaring thus helping you tap into it. Below, you will find some of the top cryptocurrencies in the world, enjoy the read.

1. Bitcoin (BTC)

This is the first and most popular cryptocurrency released in the year 2009, it works pretty much without a central bank and relies on the peer-to-peer system of the transaction which takes place between users. With Bitcoins, there are no intermediaries or middlemen, and the transactions are verified via the network nodes with the help of cryptography thus ensuring the safety of transactions. The records of purchases made with Bitcoin are in a public ledger referred to as the "blockchain" You can exchange Bitcoins for other products, currencies and services as it is currently the most accepted cryptocurrency worldwide

.

2. Litecoin (LTC)

Litecoin was released in the year 2011; it quickly followed the release of the Bitcoin. If individuals referred to Bitcoin as the gold of cryptocurrency, then Litecoin is the silver because it has also enjoyed some measure of success regarding the growth rate of merchants who are willing to invest. This cryptocurrency operates an open source global payment network that isn't supervised by any central body Litecoin as a digital currency is just like the Bitcoin.

However, its block generation process makes its transaction confirmation rate faster than that of the Bitcoin.

3. Ripple(XRP)

If you are looking for a global settlement network that provides low-cost international payment, then Ripple is your best bet. The significant difference between this crypto coin and Bitcoin lies in the fact that unlike Bitcoins, there are no mining processes required. Because they do not require mining, the level of computing power is reduced thus increasing their network protection. Ripple's focus on business development deals has enhanced the spread of their coins thus drawing the attention of institutional and international buyers.

4. Ethereum (ETH)

Right after the world still reels off the impact of Bitcoin and Ripple, Ethereum launched on the scene in 2015. Ethereum is a platform that is run on distributed applications without any fraud nor interference from third parties. It has its cryptographic token known as ether; so if a developer seeks to run applications in Ethereum, they will have to get Ether. This cryptocurrency has the second highest market capitalization after Bitcoin which is over $41 billion. The Ether can be very useful in codifying, decentralization, securing and trading anything! With the Ethereum, you certainly get the whole package.

5. Zcash (ZEC)

2016 came with a bang as the world witnessed the launch of Zcash, I like to say that this digital coin holds a lot of promise because it has an array of features that are appealing to investors. The most significant fear of most individuals who invest in cryptocurrency is usually fear of losing sensitive information to hackers, however, with

Zcash, you can rest easy knowing that your details are protected. Details such as recipient, sender and amount are kept private thus shielding transaction information. Content is also encrypted as a measure put in place to aid protection.

6. Dash

If you want to carry out your transaction that would not be traceable, then this cryptocurrency is for you. Dash is a secretive version of Bitcoin as such whatever transactions you carry out via this currency will be nearly untraceable. Launched in 2014, Dash has enjoyed the followership of individuals who seek to keep their cryptocurrencies in secret. This coin can be mined, and the team behind its creation keeps strategizing on ways to keep it ahead of its contemporaries thus it can be said that the coin has got potential for sustainability.

7. Monero (XMR)

Donation-based and community-driven are just some of the words to use in describing this crypto coin. Launched in April 2014, the Monero has become a cryptocurrency investor's delight; it is private, untraceable and very secure. With its unique technique known as the "ring signature", you can observe a lot of signatures (cryptographic of course) with a real one hidden between, however, the signatures will all appear real, so it becomes tough to isolate the authentic one. This measure put in place gives this digital coin an advantage over others.

There you have it, my top seven cryptocurrencies you can take advantage of in this season. Remember that these coins vary from one to another, they are all cryptocurrencies yet unique in their way. Bitcoins remain the leading crypto coins regarding market maximization, popularity, value and customer base but other coins such as Ripple and Ethereum are gradually gaining ground and becoming the favorite as well. In the last chapter of this book, we will discuss on the future of cryptocurrencies and how this growing competition might work out in the nearest future. You know what cryptocurrencies are and now you see the various types available, it's time to take the plunge by investing! Find out more in the next chapter.

Chapter Three

Top Steps on how to Invest in Cryptocurrency

Before we dive into the world of "skyrocketing" prices and bubbles "popping" by the hour, you have to remember this golden rule because it will save you a lot of headaches and disappointments.

"Never compare crypto bubbles with traditional financial bubbles. 10 percent up is not a bubble but can be daily volatility. 100 percent up can be a bubble, but often it is just the start of it. 1,000 percent might be a bubble usually, but there is no guarantee that it pops,,

With all that you have learnt thus far, you should be willing to take the plunge in and invest in cryptocurrencies because it is a risk that will most likely yield good results if the investment is done right. Investing in cryptocurrency is a huge risk, make no mistakes about that, but if you study the market well enough, have the right information backed by an excellent crypto coin, you can be sure that your investment will hit the right spot and produce good fruits for you.

Below, you will find my top tips on how to invest in cryptocurrency, these steps have been tested and used over and over again to ascertain their effectiveness, and you don't have to worry about anything concerning your investment if you follow through with all that you learn here. Ready?

1. Understand the Market

Just like every other investment market, it is essential that you understand what you are getting into before you begin. The first chapters of this book have helped you prepare for this moment, but you can gain more knowledge. Investing in cryptocurrency is very risky so don't expect a walk in the park. You've got to understand that it comes with a lot of risks. **Be** aware of the "Pump and Dump" which is illegal but federal agencies do not actively protect cryptocurrency. Pump and dump scams involve two groups of people. First there are the players who artificially increase the price of a coin by promoting or endorsing it. They've spent several minutes, hours or even days buying up cheap coins, and when they are ready to dump them, they build up the buzz. As buzz around the coin gains momentum, trading volume increase and the coins value goes up. You are both the pump and dumper. Once the coin hits a desired price the players sell all their coins, and people begin to panic sell, dumping their coins on the market and sending the price plummeting.

Understanding the market also means you are always one step ahead of the news; by monitoring, researching and gaining information about what needs to be at every time. If you are proactive enough, nothing will successfully take you by surprise. So there you have it, the very step to investing; understand the marketplace!

2. Buying Coins

First Level: Invest only in Tier 1 currencies

Your journey in the world of cryptocurrencies it's about to begin. Do the following steps:

1. Register for Coinbase

2. Submit identity verification

3. Setup funding account, use bank for lowest fees

4. Download the Coinbase mobile app

5. As a beginner you'll want to invest in Tier 1 currencies, they are the safest cryptocurrency and highly unlikely to be dumped and forgotten.

Always begin with [Coinbase](#) it's tested, verified and is the safest and most secure online cryptocurrency site. You can be reasonably confident that your bank and personal information is secure there.

When you begin building up your portfolio with different cryptocurrencies your first investment should be spread between the three Tier 1 currencies in this order: 45% Bitcoin (BTC), 35% Ethereum (ETC), 20% Litecoin (LTC). I personally found success in purely investing all of my money in Bitcoin but as a beginner that would be reckless because the crypto market is highly volatile and the price can plummet at any time. Start with a reasonably small investment of cryptocurrency to get your bearings. For example, if you transferred 800$ start with investing 500$ and keep the rest in case you need them later because you never want to invest everything you have. Now go to the chart of each currency and check the 24hour window, note that lowest value listed and make an excel spreadsheet, write it down and add 20-30% to that price, that will be your sign when to buy. If you have the Coinbase mobile app setup alerts to trigger when the currency value is close to the one you wrote down in the spreadsheet.

3. Long-term investing and DCA

Before you make your first investment we'll take a look at DCA and the benefits you gain especially if you are a beginner. Dollar Cost Averaging, or DCA for short, is "an investment technique of buying a fixed dollar amount of a particular investment on a regular schedule, regardless of share price." This is a technique used by both traditional investors (stocks, etc) and by cryptocurrency investors to reduce risk. By purchasing a financial instrument regularly, you average the price you bought at—if the value of the instrument goes up, so does your gain. If the value goes down, your average price invested goes down as well, so you are down less money than if you had invested everything at one price. This is especially important when investing in something as volatile and risky as Bitcoin. By dividing the total sum to be invested in the market, in our case 500$ into equal amounts put into the market at regular intervals (500$ over 6 weeks). DCA hopes to reduce the risk of incurring a substantial loss on markets undergoing temporary decline because it exposes only part of the total sum to the decline. If you are going to follow the DCA route you'll want to start your first week with an investment of 83$ which equals to 37,35$ into BTC, 29,05$ into ETC and 16,6$ into LTC if you want to increase your profit margins by reducing your spending on the Coinbase fees you'll want to use GDAX which is the sister site of Coinbase. You can directly use your Coinbase account on GDAX but the fees when you make a purchase or sell are much lower (0.25% compared to 1.5% on Coinbase) the trade-off is having to deal with more advanced interface. After you made your purchase now it's time to sit back and watch the chart, keep in mind that no one has ever successfully timed the market over multiple stocks and the crypto market is no different. Avoid day trading and trying to "guess" the highs and lows because the cryptocurrencies are highly volatile and the price can plummet at any time it's a Russian roulette with zeros and ones. The risk will always be high but it comes with a high reward if you are here for the long-term. If you have success and the prices went up repeat the same every week and invest accordingly to the formula.

3. Investing in Altcoins

Second Level: Tier 2 currency

Before we talk about investing in Altcoins let's take a look at what exactly is an Altcoin. Alternative coins or Altcoins for short are cryptocurrencies that came into the limelight after the successful launch of the Bitcoin. Essentially, all cryptocurrencies run on the Blockchain and operate on the same mode as Bitcoins. They are conceived as alternatives of Bitcoin and make use of the inadequacies of the Bitcoin. Altcoins like Bitcoin are peer-to-peer currency that thrives on the mining process because the lower difficulty which allows for more coins to be mined at lower hash rate. With the introduction of Altcoins things like transaction speed, DNS resolution, proof-of-stake and many more became better and faster. They can also differ from Bitcoin in a few ways:

1. **Economical**: Some coins may have more of a logical economic roadmap with a quite limited amount of coins like Ripple(XRP) which is a centralized system and they can't be mined, while other coins may be mined easily, and have more coins available which leads to a bigger market cap.

2. **Coin distribution:** Coins like Ripple as mentioned before cannot be mined and the only source is if the company that owns Ripple to release more on the market. Some Altcoins have controlled mining, while others were distributed evenly to everyone in the country that coin was created. Most common altcoins with a big market cap are Dash, Dogecoin, Ripple, Zcash and Monero. Before an Altcoin is available on the market they are launched with an Initial Coin Offering or ICO for short. During ICO, Altcoins are much cheaper than their usual market price, the sales window for such events is mostly broken down to into three or more phases, with bonus levels reducing with each stage. While the first stage might attract 30 percent bonus, the last stage might be down to 5 percent or zero bonus.

Since Coinbase doesn't offer Altcoins you can use one of the following exchanges who are verified and trusted: [Bittrex](), [Bitfinex](), [Poloniex](). Be aware Altcoins are way more volatile but the rewards are greater because as an example Dash was sold for only 1$ per coin back in 2014 but last year in December, Dash hit the price mark of 1,177$ per coin registering an increase of 117,000%!

4. Follow the rules of investing

These rules are just my examples from personal experience and the disappointments I had.

1. **Never sell/buy based on emotions -** The price of Bitcoin is falling down and all you see is people selling their crypto assets? Don't panic and stay calm I've heard a lot of stories of people selling when the price drops just to find out that it was just temporary and see the price going up.

Or buying when the price is high because they are afraid of missing out. Don't make this mistake because if you truly believe in your investment and you are here for the long-run then temporary price fluctuations don't matter. If the price starts to drop don't sell your coins but wait for the drop to stop and then buy more coins which you can sell later when the price goes up!

2. **Invest only what you are ready to lose** - This goes without saying, but I can't stress it enough when talking to other people who want to start investing. Don't throw all your college savings, salary or retirement money just to watch it disappear on the Crypto Market and get nothing in return besides restless nights and headaches. The optimal amount you can invest is 7-15% of your income but if you can't handle losing some of your money on the Crypto Market then you shouldn't invest.

3. Diversify your investments – There's the saying "Don't put all your eggs in one basket" and it applies here too. Don't go all out on a single coin like Bitcoin or Ethereum just to see its price plummet or go stale for months, always try to look for new coins and invest in them if you want to make it simple write down in a spread sheet your top 10 coins and start investing. But make sure you put a bigger percentage of your budget on safer coins like Bitcoin, Ethereum, Litecoin.

Ready to invest now? I'm sure you are! By taking these steps to heart, you will be setting yourself up for massive wins concerning your investment. As much as there are many ways to do things, also remember that there are many ways of doing things the right way. The steps you find above will strategically reposition you as an investment guru in the world of cryptocurrency. Take them seriously, and you wouldn't have to worry about the money you throw into investing. The next chapter highlights the steps you can take in protecting and sharing your digital coins; after taking the bold step to gain knowledge and invest in crypto coins, you've got to learn how to protect your investment, I shouldn't give it all away here so flip over to the next chapter and learn.

Chapter Four
How to protect and share Cryptocurrency

As you invest, it is essential that you understand that cryptocurrencies are susceptible to hacks and other online related issues so safety should be a priority. This chapter seeks to reveal the best ways through which you can protect your crypto coins and also get to share them with individuals. There are levels and steps to take when analyzing cryptocurrency; it doesn't stop at knowing about the coins nor knowing how to invest; you got to know every tiny detail and safety trumps every other thing. This chapter will be split in two; the first part will focus on the top ways you can secure your coins and the second part will be focused on how you can share your crypto coins.

Before talking about the best ways to save your coins, I want you to know that the safest way to store your coins is by keeping them in wallets. It could be online or hardware wallets, but the main issue is to have a safe wallet. So in this chapter, we will discover the best wallets you can keep your coins and go to bed knowing that your coins are safe. Ready?

The Best Wallets to Keep your Coins Safe

1. Coinbase

This is an online wallet that is the beginner version of GDAX. You can transfer to the GDAX exchange for free within the same interface. Also, your crypto holdings on Coinbase are insured, and you can utilize the Coinbase vault if you want a more secure outlet for your coins. What this online wallet offers cuts across both opportunities that can secure your coins and give you free access to services that will help you grow your coins. However, you have to know that Coinbase only accommodates Bitcoin and Ethereum thus you will be restricted to these coins, there are the leading coins in the world, so you are in safe hands.

2. Nano Ledger S-

This is also a secure way of saving coins at a very low price. Sometimes people consider the cost when seeking wallets to store coins; there is no point in keeping little coins and paying huge fees. In addition to looking for a wallet that is secure, individuals also look for wallets whose services aren't so pricey. With the Nano ledger S, you get affordability and security It is a hardware wallet that is quite small thus making it very easy to carry around, you can purchase this wallet for as low as $65; what are you waiting for then? Get it, start saving and make way for investments!

3. **KeepKey**

This is a hardware wallet that has come to make a statement in the world of crypto wallets. With sleek designs and amazing material components, this wallet is a must-have for the financial individual who is passionate about making money yet keen on purchasing quality wallets. It is often referred to as a premium wallet which is a bit heavy but has a simple UI for clients that is standard for all their wallets. Firmness, sleek designs and a protective outlook, your coins can be tucked safely away from theft.

4. **Trezor**

Also a hardware wallet, Trezor is one of the leading manufacturers when it comes to hardware as such, you will be relying on their years of experience as well as top-notch security. With Trezor, you get more of a vault than a wallet;

you will be protected from virtual and physical theft. If you can say how some kernel you will be buying.

5. MyEtherWallet

You don't have to bring out cash all the time because thus crypto is a paper wallet. The money you save from this process can be used to further in your coins, all you need to do to get one is to visit myetherwallet.com and as you do, take note of the unique keys. If you are sceptical about the online version, then you can download the offline version. Also, paper wallets are free, but you have to know what you are doing for you to reap the benefits, I will not advise beginners to take on this kind of wallet as it requires a lot of teaching and issues. My Ether Wallet is for the person who has studied everything about crypto coins and has narrowed down his/her decision to this one.

6. Jaxx

With an array of versions now available, this online wallet was the first digital clock. It has versions on Android, desktop and browser, allow you receive funds, scan QR code, view your crypto holding and much more, all in one app. This is a promising solution, but because it has a lot of integrations, it might take a while to learn the unique features and use them

.7. Electrum

Mobile users can bank on this online wallet as it can be used on the desktop as well. It is quite flexible, and the best part is that you can achieve anonymity with it as well as use its hardware wallets if you want to. The Electrum is connected to several servers as such; you will most likely not experience a server downtime. Try out this wallet and be grateful you did.

The best ways to share your crypto coins

1. **GDAX**: This is a process through which the sender doesn't get to pay a dime for transferring coins if it is connected to Coinbase; there is a standard fee of 0.25% for takers and 0% for senders. It is an easy way to share coins, and I'm sure you will have fun with it.

2. **Kraken:** This exchange platform offers the highest fees but they are trustworthy, and you can rely on this platform for a decent transfer of coins. However, if you share a certain amount of coins then the high fees can be reduced, so you get a fair deal with a certain amount of security that comes with dealing with a trusted platform.

3. **Poloniex**: With Poloniex, you get offers for coins which can be utilized for trading. Here's the best part; the taker pays 0.25% while the maker pays 0.15%. It is the most convenient payment option that helps you share your coins.

This chapter has been all about the best ways to protect your crypto coins as well as share them at the slightest fees. You can be sure that your coins wouldn't be at risk if you keep to these simple safety wallets You can also share your coins with the tips shared here. The next chapter takes things up a notch by focusing on the future of cryptocurrency, what does the future hold for the digital coins? Find out.

Chapter Five

Introduction to Mining

The core of mining is the idea of block rewards. For most coins, these are given to the person/group that finds a valid solution to the cryptographic hashing algorithm. This solution is a mathematical calculation that uses the results of previous block solutions, so there's no way to pre-calculate answers for a future block without knowing the solution to the previous block. This history of block solutions and transactions creates the blockchain that is in the core of cryptocurrencies which is a sort of public ledger. The block contains cryptographic signatures or the block and the transactions within the block. The transactions are collected from the network, typically with a small fee attached, which also becomes part of the block reward. There's a difficulty value attached to the solution for a block as well, which can scale up/down over time, the goal being to keep the rate of generation of new blocks relatively constant. The target for Bitcoin miners is to generate a block solution every 10 minutes on average while other cryptocurrencies like Ethereum have an average block generation of 16 seconds which is obviously a huge reason why some people favor Ethereum than Bitcoin. To make the introduction simple the number solution has to be lower than some value. The solution includes the wallet address for the solving system, which then receives all the transaction fees along with the block reward, and the block gets written to the blockchain of all participating systems also known as a mining pool.

Mining Pools

As a miner, you can mine as an individual or you can join a group of miners also known as a mining pool and work together to solve solutions. The mining pool acts like a individual miner, but actually it's comprised of hundreds of other individual miners. They share their mining rigs processing power and work together towards solving a solution in order to generate a block as a reward of solving a particular problem. After that the mining pool gives the miners their share of the reward depending on the computer power also known as hash rate TH/s they contributed to the solving process. There are different mining pools for each cryptocurrency and they have different rewards percentage, most known ones are: **Slush Pool** - They are the oldest mining pool in existence with worldwide servers, currently they represent 11.4% of the total hash power used across all mining pools. The pool fees are relatively high in comparison with other mining pools standing at 2%. **AntPool** - AntPool is the largest currently operating mining pool in the world with a unique feature that gives their miners the option to choose how they want to be rewarded. First method is PPS (Payment Per Share) which means you're charged 4% on pay-outs plus 2% of any transaction fees earned. You can also choose PPLNS (Payment Per Last N Shares) which is free but AntPool will keep all transaction fees. They also represent over a quarter of the total hash power but the down side is the payouts on AntPool are smaller compared to other mining pools. **BTC.com** - BTC is one of the most well-known brands they became famous for their powerful Bitcoin wallet and having their own blockchain explorer. They also have their own method of rewarding miners known as FPPS (Full Pay Per Share). FPPS calculates a standard transaction fee within a given period, adds it to the block reward (currently 12.5 BTC) and then distributes the whole to miners as with traditional PPS (Payment Per Share). The only issue they have is their rather flaky website which sometimes fails to load or crashes.

Mining Hardware

In the early days, miners used their central processing unit (CPU) to mine, but soon this wasn't fast enough and it bogged down the system resources of the host computer. Miners quickly moved on to using the graphical processing unit (GPU) in computer graphics cards because they were able to hash data 50 to 100 times faster and consumed much less power per unit of work. Back in 2011 a new industry sprang with custom made CPU's made specifically for mining this pushed the performance standards even higher. The first custom made CPUs are known as (FPGA), they used much less power than the standard GPU's and

CPU's and made mining farms possible for the first time. Application-specific integrated circuit or ASIC miners have taken over completely. These ASIC machines mine at unprecedented speeds while consuming much less power than FPGA or GPU mining rigs. Several reputable companies have established themselves with excellent products with AntMiner being at the top.

Chapter Six

The future of Cryptocurrency

With all that you have learnt thus far, what do you think about cryptocurrency in the nearest future? Do you believe it will remain relevant or do you doubt its sustainability? It isn't enough to know all about investing alone; you've got to know if this venture is worth the risk and if it has a bright future as well. This chapter seeks to help you understand what the future holds for crypto coins and how you can plan as an individual towards either the acquisition of more coins or selling off your coins for better investment options.

Firstly, the massive acceptance level of cryptocurrencies all around the world is an indication that this digital currency has gained the trust of a large crowd. So many people now organize and execute their seminars and training on cryptocurrencies, and there are large crowds who turn up to listen as well thus showing that there is acceptance. Now, with this level of recognition, you can be sure that for a very long time, cryptocurrencies will be on the lips of several people because a lot of people believe that it is the key to sustainable digital wealth. If you want to determine if something has a good future, then check if it has the number of people needed to drive the message; concerning crypto coins, the number is on the increase, so cash in now and plan for the future.

Furthermore, cryptocurrencies are backed by the steady backbone of technology which isn't going away anytime soon. So long we've got the internet, then we have a way of trading and buying. The better technology gets by the day, the better your experience with digital coins. This is one feature to always look for when considering the future of a business or sector; is the platform sustainable? Can it stand the test of time? Although cryptocurrencies are volatile, technology as a platform for them will always be a steady backbone that can be trusted, at least you know you can carry out your transactions anywhere, anytime and with the right device.

Money is in an ever-evolving stage as such; you can never actually tell if a particular currency will be as valuable as it is now in the future. With cryptocurrency, however, you can be sure that it will be a part of our future because the world is gradually tilting towards more technology defined payment plans rather than cash. Look around you today, see the automated teller machines, the fast ways through which monies can be sent via the internet, the reliance on this method of monetary transfer tells one that gradually the world is becoming more accepting of unconventional ways of using the money. As of today, there are few retail shops (online and offline) who accept cryptocurrencies, the stores who do not accept are more than those who do but here's the good news, there were no stores accepting in the beginning. It was a gradual process that has now built up to some stores and eventually it will be a lot of stores. So you see, the future already made way for crypto coins, you just need to accept it.

The business you do with cryptocurrencies are instant, and they have a global appeal so that you can be in one country and trade with someone else in another continent. The distance doesn't hinder the process either does it affect the transaction. So you can be sure that over time, you can make very fast operations that have a global appeal and involve persons that aren't just within your sphere of contact. You can experience swift transactions with someone in your office and still experience the same level of the swiftness with someone abroad, in the past, this wasn't so easy neither was it possible a sit sometimes required some days for verification and all. With cryptocurrency, you can enjoy instant and global reach; I say the future is bright.

The presence of cryptography in transactions makes it extremely secure. It is almost impossible to break in because of the strong cryptography used to secure the system. Money in the future is not going to be about "where" or "how" rather, it will be about the level of security offered. The questions people will ask will be about security and cryptocurrency is safe thus more people will want to trade in and invest. Cryptographic mechanism put in place will help put the right measures that eliminate the fear of the system failing.

Because there are no central controlling powers, people are thrilled by the level of independence they get with their transactions, so you know you are %100 responsible for what happens to your coins. There is no one at the top to hold responsible nor complain about pulling strings, all you have to do is download software (which is also free) and send/receive Bitcoins or any other crypto coins using the software. So easy and simple that the future is extremely excited about the continual emergence of crypto coins. You can decide what to do with the coins and build a portfolio based on what your decisions.

This chapter has brought you closer to understanding the future of cryptocurrency. From what you have read here, it is safe to say that the future is bright for cryptocurrencies. There will be volatile times and issues with the upward-downward movement of the coins but be rest assured that digital coins aren't going away just yet as they are going to get better with new variants launched and better ways of investing as well. If you believe in this crypto coins movement, then you need to take the plunge because the future is now.

Conclusion

We have been on a digital journey into the world of cryptocurrencies, and I believe you have been learning, growing and developing your mindset for the great potentials that lie within investing in crypto coins. You cannot get it wrong with cryptocurrencies when you are armed with the best information; you also cannot get it wrong when have been given everything you need to know about this aspect of digital coins. What you need to do now is start using what you have gleaned to achieve profit.

There were various aspects of this book that helped provide answers to your questions, so are you ready to go ahead and do better now?

We started by talking about cryptocurrency is all about, you gained an in-depth understanding of what the coins are about, how you can trade, the volatility level and how the currency operates. This first chapter served as the foundation on which other aspects are built on. We went on to discuss the types of crypto coins available, and I'm sure you got to know the type of coins that were available in the market. Knowing the types will help you narrow down your choice and also give you a better perspective on the coins that are good for investments and the ones that aren't strong enough.

Learning about how to invest in crypto coins was also addressed; the essence of this book is not just to present the information you need to know, but to present the information you need to take decisive steps that bring about change in your investment portfolios. So after learning what crypto coins are the next best step to take is how to invest, you've to start thinking about how this book brings value to your life and investment is the way forward. When you start investing, you've got to think about security as well; are your funds secure? Do you have a place to keep them till they are needed? These are questions that led to the inclusion of the chapter that focuses on how to secure your coins. Get the best online or offline wallets, and you can be sure that your coins wouldn't be exposed to theft and the likes.

Whatever we do now resonate onto the future, so the last chapter that focuses on cryptocurrency and the future helps remind you of the fact that the future is bright for crypto coins, but you have got to be willing to take it and make it a part of your life. So many opportunities abound for the one who is willing to take cryptocurrencies to another level, and the future is ready for you so hold on tight, and you will never have to look back with regrets. Putting this book together has been the most fantastic experience for me, thank you for allowing me to share the knowledge with you and also thank you for taking the right steps that promise positive results, your experience with cryptocurrency will never be the same again as with new information comes great strides and great progress.

Quick Reminder If You Have Missed Your Gift!

https://www.subscribepage.com/bitcoin-for-beginners

Welcome to the last page reader, I'm happy to see you here I hope you had a great experience reading my first book and if you want to support my work you are welcome to share your thoughts and leave a review.

Respectfully,
William B. Skates